PETER COOK graduated from the Victorian College of the Arts in 2001. As an actor, his theatre credits include *Cigarettes and Chocolate* for Darlinghurst Theatre; *Europe*, *The Removalists* and The QLD Premiers Drama Awards for Queensland Theatre Company; *The Eisteddfod*, *Breathing Corpses* and *The Chain Bridge* for The Street, Canberra; *Wet and Dry* for NIDA; *Anatomy Titus Fall of Rome* for Queensland Theatre Company/Bell Shakespeare; *Tender* for Metro Arts, Brisbane; and *Breaking The Castle* for The Street, HotHouse Theatre, Riverside Theatres and QPAC. His TV credits include *All Saints*, *Young Lions*, *Terra Nova*, *Redfern Now*, *The Gods of Wheat Street*, *Secrets and Lies*, *Old School*, *The Secret Daughter*, *Home and Away* and *Total Control*. His feature film credits include *Danny Deckchair*, *Down Under Mystery Tour* and *Beauty and the Beast*. Peter has worked extensively in the field of theatre in education over the past ten years, writing work with young people across the country. *Breaking The Castle* is his debut as a playwright. He also wrote for the *Dear Australia* project run by PlayWriting Australia.

# BREAKING THE CASTLE

Peter Cook

**CURRENCY PRESS**
The performing arts publisher

CURRENCY PLAYS

First published in 2021
by Currency Press Pty Ltd,
PO Box 2287, Strawberry Hills, NSW, 2012, Australia
enquiries@currency.com.au
www.currency.com.au

This revised edition first published in 2023.

Copyright: *Breaking the Castle* © Peter Cook, 2020, 2021, 2023.

COPYING FOR EDUCATIONAL PURPOSES

The Australian *Copyright Act 1968* (Act) allows a maximum of one chapter or 10% of this book, whichever is the greater, to be copied by any educational institution for its educational purposes provided that that educational institution (or the body that administers it) has given a remuneration notice to Copyright Agency (CA) under the Act.

For details of the CA licence for educational institutions contact CA, 12/66 Goulburn Street, Sydney, NSW, 2000; tel: within Australia 1800 066 844 toll free; outside Australia 61 2 9394 7600; fax: 61 2 9394 7601; email: memberservices@copyright.com.au

COPYING FOR OTHER PURPOSES

Except as permitted under the Act, for example a fair dealing for the purposes of study, research, criticism or review, no part of this book may be reproduced, stored in a retrieval system, or transmitted in any form or by any means without prior written permission. All enquiries should be made to the publisher at the address above.

Any performance or public reading of *Breaking the Castle* is forbidden unless a licence has been received from the author or the author's agent. The purchase of this book in no way gives the purchaser the right to perform the play in public, whether by means of a staged production or a reading. All applications for public performance should be addressed to the author c/- Currency Press.

Typeset by Dean Nottle for Currency Press.
Cover features Peter Cook.
Cover photo by Grant Leslie. Design by Mathias Johansson for Currency Press.

Currency Press acknowledges the Traditional Owners of the Country on which we live and work. We pay our respects to all Aboriginal and Torres Strait Islander Elders, past and present.

 A catalogue record for this book is available from the National Library of Australia

# Contents

*Foreword*     vii

*Writer's note*     ix

BREAKING THE CASTLE     1

# Foreword

When I first meet Peter Cook, or Pete as he prefers to be called, he tells me he is excited but nervous. 'I'm good mate, but yeah I'm a bit nervous!'

The next day, his extraordinary one-man play, *Breaking the Castle* will open its first Sydney season at Riverside Theatres, Parramatta. Almost like Dave Smith, his protagonist, Pete is edgy, and excited, and yep, 'pretty fucken nervous!'

These nerves prove wasted as Pete takes the stage. Just 24 hours later he inhabits a range of visceral and very real characters through his performance. His authentic storytelling touched me and the audience in unique, personal and often unexpected ways, culminating in a rousing standing ovation at its conclusion.

Pete's story is not pretty. It is at times harsh in content and delivery yet, at the same time, poetic and lyrical. Through Dave Smith, Pete shares his story of addiction and ultimate redemption. This is a road hard fought and filled with pain through loss, isolation and self-doubt. We are invited to intimately experience his painful journey, and be confronted by the moments that have brought him to this dark place, the walls of his 'castle' that imprisoned, rather than protected him.

Getting to know Pete over a number of chats and coffees, I was struck by his ability to avidly listen and observe people accurately. His trauma is writ large in the words of this play, yet the man I befriended bears no resentment, no evidence of his accumulated scars. Rather, Pete exudes calm and a reassuring presence tinged with a joyful and boyish charm.

After the success of its premiere season at The Street in Canberra, Riverside first presented *Breaking the Castle* as our theatre emerged from the January 2022 Omicron wave which trashed the summer season for Sydney theatres. This was a time that challenged not just our industry, but all people and their ways of living. We all navigated personal and family challenges in this period and since that time have seen a society-wide explosion of depression and anxiety, particularly in our children and young people.

Sadly, we have seen a significant increase in many forms of addiction. Understandably, many who experienced loss and fear found solace in whatever helped get them through the day, whatever helped dull or relieve their pain.

Works such as *Breaking The Castle* are important. They address real issues in a relatable way sharing the message that you are not broken; you are not alone. Raw, direct and honest delivery of positive messages contained in this and other artistic works can cut through in a 'no bullshit' way for young audiences. This is far more effective than any government program, public health brochure, or accusatory and punitive approach.

In this context, the message of *Breaking the Castle* is as relevant and important today as it was when Pete's personal journey began. Addiction is not a weakness, or even an illness. It is most often a response to the pain and sadness of trauma or depression. Those living with addiction should not earn our judgement but rather our support, kindness and patience.

We all build our 'castles', hoping that the walls we build will protect us and save us from more trauma, but often find these same walls becoming the dark prisons that we need to escape from to find the light again.

For me, this is the message of Pete's story and *Breaking the Castle*. We all experience times of frailty when we need the help of others. We make mistakes, we trip, we fall and, for some, getting up is just too damned hard. All it takes is just one good person to accept us without judgement or derision, who is prepared to reach out a hand with kindness and help us find our way back home.

I am in in awe of Pete's courage, determination and brutal honesty, and I am proud to call him my mate. It's impossible not to admire a person who has developed such wonderful work, and who is so committed to sharing his message of hope and redemption, no matter how 'fucken nervous' he may still get!

It's one helluva story and he's a helluva bloke.

*Craig McMaster*
*Director, Riverside Theatres Parramatta*

## Writer's note

*Breaking the Castle* is based on my story, but it's also a universal story about how those of us who struggle with trauma and mental illness can find ourselves in active addiction.

From the streets of Kings Cross where I lived among those using daily, to the rehabilitation centre in Thailand where I started my recovery process, I learned that the factors contributing to addiction are the same across the globe. I wrote this play because I got lucky, my rehab was paid for, and while in rehab I realised that I was one of a very small percentage who make it out alive. Most people, especially those on the fringes without access to resources, will never have that chance, especially under current policy in Australia, and I wanted to give them a voice. I also wrote it to take away some of the stigma that still surrounds addiction and mental health, to create a sense of understanding about the causes leading to addiction, but most importantly to humanise people suffering with this disease and to encourage a sense of compassion for those who have fallen between the cracks.

The play has now had three seasons; the world premiere was at The Street Theatre in Canberra in 2020. The day after our closing night the country went into its very first lockdown because of the pandemic, but the work survived COVID, managing seasons at HotHouse Theatre in Albury in 2021, Riverside Theatres in Parramatta in 2022 and, as I write, we are only six weeks away from opening night at QPAC in 2023.

The response to the play from audiences has literally been overwhelming. I have had people say to me that they will never look at addiction the same way again, people telling me their life has been changed after seeing the work, family members of people suffering with addiction thanking me for sharing my story with them, people letting me know that because of this work they can now understand their loved ones on a deeper level and find more empathy for people they know who are suffering with addiction and mental health issues. The response has let me know that audiences are connecting with the work and that it speaks to people from all walks of life. It cuts across class, gender and race because it's a play about being human, about looking for the humanity in others, and about the importance of human connection. Things we can all relate to. I want to go to the theatre to be moved, to be changed, to be challenged, and I believe *Breaking The Castle* does this. Without fail, every single time I have performed this show people have laughed and cried and I can't ask anything more of myself or the work than that. I hope I have the privilege to keep performing the show for years to come.

I need to thank Caroline Stacey and Shelly Higgs at The Street for developing the work and programming it, Karla Conway at HotHouse Theatre, Sophie Clausen, Catherine Swallow and Craig McMaster at Riverside Theatres, Jono Perry at QPAC for having the vision to bring it to Brisbane and my great friends Leah Purcell and Bain Stewart for directing and producing the work in its next life at QPAC.

Thank you to whoever is reading this. I hope you remember to look at the butterflies.

Peace.

*Peter Cook*
*January 2023*

*For Sam Henderson—an unlikely angel who saved my life, my sister Louise who I still think about every day and, of course, my mum and dad.*

*Mum, you now have a son who is a playwright.*

*Breaking the Castle* was first produced by The Street and performed at The Street Theatre, Canberra, on 28 February 2020, with the following cast:

    DAVE                           Peter Cook

Director, Caroline Stacey
Set and Costume Design, Imogen Keen
Lighting Designer, Gerry Corcoran
Sound Designer, Kimmo Vennonen
Stage Manager, Kitty Malam
Dramaturgs, Caroline Stacey and Shelly Higgs

**SPECIAL THANKS**

In alphabetical order:

Jeremy Ambrum, Virginia Cook, Nicholas Cook, Michael Cook, Phoebe Cook, Helen Cook, Kim Durack, Dean Ellis, Brendan Grice, Kristian Kelly, Samantha Kelly, Marcus Kelson, Luke Meldon, Anna Morrison, Erin Mullen, Alex Natera, Maria Natera, Stephen Phillips, Leah Purcell, Conor Reid, Patricia Shankar, Bain Stewart, Ursula Yovich, and the whole Hartney clan.

# CHARACTERS

In order of appearance:

DAVID SMITH, 35-40 years old, an actor
JOHNNY, a man David used to do drugs with
COUNSELLOR, a counsellor in rehab, from the East End, London
AMERICAN MAN, an American man in rehab
SOUTH AFRICAN MAN, a man from South Africa in rehab
IRISHMAN, a man from Ireland in rehab
MIDDLE-EASTERN WOMAN, a woman from Qatar in rehab
GERMAN LADY, a woman from Germany in rehab
NORWEGIAN WOMAN, a woman from Norway in rehab
CRITIC, Dave's inner critic
ADDICT, Dave's inner addict
HER, a woman in Kings Cross
BLOKE, a middle-aged punter in a TAB
RACING COMMENTATOR, a horse race caller
CASTING AGENT, a 19-year-old male casting agent
COACH, an older high school football coach
MOTHER, Dave's mother when he was a boy
FATHER, Dave's father when he was a boy
DIRECTOR, a female theatre director
COP, a policeman in Kings Cross
DOCTOR, an emergency department doctor
NURSE, a nurse in the psychiatric ward
PATIENT, a schizophrenic patient in the psychiatric ward
FRANK, Dave's best friend of twenty years
JOHNNY'S GIRLFRIEND, a woman David used to do drugs with

*Breaking the Castle* was originally performed with one actor playing all roles, except where it is specified in the script there is a voice-over. The characters can be played by any number of actors or voice-overs could be used for all of them.

Diversity Pledge:

I encourage anyone producing and casting this work to consider performers and creatives from diverse backgrounds especially where a character's ethnic or cultural background, age, sexuality, gender or disability need not be specified.

# SETTING

The play moves through the various worlds and states of being that David experiences. The stage and set should have the capacity to blend all his worlds and his state of mind.

In the world of the couch there is an overflowing ashtray, wine and vodka bottles, some empty, some half full—glasses on the ground, takeaway containers with food still in them, chocolate wrappers, plays by Shakespeare, other classic modern plays, newspapers, and a pair of women's underpants or a bra lie on the floor. There can also be empty zip bags from cocaine, alfoil and other remnants of drug paraphernalia. There is an old football and piles of clothes scattered throughout.

The world of rehab should feel spacious, lush, and inspired by nature. It's also orderly—a hospital surrounded by trees and plants.

The world of the castle—the little boy's castle—or David's subconscious, can be represented in any way, through objects or through light, space and sound. The feeling of the space during the castle scenes should be sparse and empty, like a great echo chamber.

## 1. BELLY OF THE BEAST

*Backstage at the theatre.*

DAVE: I'm nervous. I'm really fucken nervous … but nerves are good. Nerves mean it's real.

I'm backstage in the theatre, in the belly of the beast. They've called beginners and I'm here waiting for my cue—it's a sound cue—and when I hear it, I'm on. When the music plays, I'm on stage and I can't wait. I love this feeling. That's my cue. I'm on.

*Now. It is early evening in Kings Cross, Sydney. Sounds of traffic, pedestrians, the faint beating of sounds from nightclubs—it's ominous—the night is beginning in the city of sin.*

Darlinghurst Road, King Cross. I'm in the belly of the beast, right in the guts of the lights, the sounds, the madness. I remember walking up and down this street all times of the day and night, lost and lonely … looking to score, looking for a girl, looking for someone, something, anything. I see all the places I used to get on. I remember the faces of the dealers. The smell of the streets. The other users. The cheap hotel rooms. The chaos. It's like reliving a nightmare.

*Beat.*

What the fuck am I doing back here?

DAVE *starts to walk away.*

JOHNNY: Dave! Dave! Is that … Oh, I knew it was you!
DAVE: Hey, Johnny.
JOHNNY: Where you been, bro, thought you musta got locked up, or died or something?
DAVE: I've been in Thailand.
JOHNNY: Thailand? You went on a plane?
DAVE: Yep.
JOHNNY: What—did ya do a run for someone or something?
DAVE: No, mate, I was in rehab.
JOHNNY: Rehab? Oh … cool, cool.

You wanna get on? I'm on my way to meet Sal down the basketball courts, yeah, getting half a ball—you want in?

DAVE: It all comes rushing back, the anticipation of getting on, the danger, the risk, the ritual. Lighting the pipe, the sound of the crystal melting, the smell of the perfumes the girls would wear, the sex, how good the high feels all through your body, the escape after that first puff. My body wants that feeling back. Just one last time ... My body wants it—more than water, food, anything, it wants that feeling now. The butterflies are in my stomach. Fuck. I want to get high. I want the drug.

JOHNNY: Dave, you coming or what?

## 2. CHECKING IN

*Rehab. One year earlier.* DAVE *sits in a chair in process group.*

COUNSELLOR: David. David? Would you like to check in?

DAVE: It's my first day of rehab. I'm in what's called process group. This is 'checking in'. It's how you start every day. Everyone has to tell the group how they feel each morning before the session starts properly.

How did my life take me here? A rehab facility in Thailand. It doesn't feel real.

The group is silent, waiting uncomfortably for me to say something.

The counsellor looks at me, 'It's okay, David, we know you've just arrived.'

I look around me at the group, it's like the United Nations of addiction. There's a Middle-Eastern woman in her forties, an Irishman with a suntan, a baby-faced American man with scars up and down his arms, an older German lady with spectacles, a young Norwegian woman, a South African bloke who looks like he's had a few beers in his life, a Malaysian lady and a few others from all corners of the globe.

The group continues to check in and I can hear what they're saying, but I'm not really listening. I hear people say things like, I feel calm, I feel hopeful. Others are depressed, homesick, flat. The group turns to me. I still can't speak.

After the check-in the floor is open. The counsellor says, 'Does anyone have any questions for our newest member?'

The group is responsible for the group process, it says on the wall.

So the group asks me questions, lots of questions.
AMERICAN MAN: When was your rock bottom, man? Huh? What's your story?
SOUTH AFRICAN MAN: What was your poison? Piss? Puff? Crank? Crack? Coke?
MIDDLE-EASTERN WOMAN: Did you have to detox at the onsite hospital?
IRISHMAN: Hey—this is rehab—we are all fucked up, you are not so special.
GERMAN LADY: We have read the group rules and you are not participating in the process.
AMERICAN MAN: You can't just say nothing, man, this is a fucken joke, what do you think, guys? Is Dave treating this group like a joke? Maybe Dave's the joke?
DAVE: This is fucken bullshit! I don't know you people; I don't have to tell you anything!
*Pause.*
NORWEGIAN WOMAN: Is this your first rehab?
DAVE: Yeah, why?
NORWEGIAN WOMAN: I know what you're going through, I was like you when I got here, I know it's difficult, but trust me, the best thing you can do is talk. Were you talking to anyone at home?
DAVE: Not lately. I was ages ago. I've seen counsellors, psychiatrists, psychologists ... I never got much out of it. I'd talk, they'd listen then I'd leave. It was never any practical help.
[*To the audience*] Actually, that's not true. One woman I saw gave me a brochure about a men's weight-loss shake. That was kind of helpful. At least I knew she thought I was overweight at the end of the session.
NORWEGIAN WOMAN: Whatever it is you've done, there's no judgement from anyone in this room.
DAVE: [*to the audience*] I take in the group; I look into all their eyes. Are they judging? Do I care?
COUNSELLOR: You alright, David?
DAVE: Yeah.
COUNSELLOR: Okay. Let's check in properly. How are you feeling today?
*Pause.*

DAVE: I feel like I want to die.
COUNSELLOR: Thank you, David. Do you think you're feeling suicidal?
DAVE: No.

[*To himself*] But I remember a few times, after taking too much, lying on the floor hoping I would die. Willing death on. Was I trying to kill myself? Maybe.

MIDDLE-EASTERN WOMAN: How long have you felt like this for?
DAVE: I can't remember not feeling like this.
COUNSELLOR: How do you feel about being in rehab?
DAVE: I'm not sure if I need to be here to be honest.
AMERICAN MAN: Well, why are you here?
DAVE: I don't know.
COUNSELLOR: How old were you when you started using?
DAVE: Fourteen.
SOUTH AFRICAN MAN: How often were you using before rehab?
DAVE: Every day.
IRISHMAN: Do you think that could be the reason you're here?
COUNSELLOR: Do you think using so heavily helps how you feel?
DAVE: Yeah. When I use I don't feel like dying.

A middle-aged Indian man, sitting next to me, who has been quiet but listening intensely the whole session, says there are worse things than dying and everyone in this room knows it.

Maybe he's right. Through a gap in the curtains, in the garden outside, I see a butterfly land on a leaf. I can't remember the last time I noticed a butterfly.

'More will be revealed,' says the counsellor to the group. I have no idea what he means.

As I'm leaving I hear my name …

COUNSELLOR: David. I want you to start writing a list of things you like about yourself.

> *The* COUNSELLOR *hands* DAVE *a notepad and pen.* DAVE *walks back to his room, discarding them both.*

DAVE: I go back to my room, I lie on my bed, I stare at the ceiling and I think.

## 3. MONDAY MORNING

*Couch world. Three months before rehab. We hear an alarm clock. He wakes up and grabs a bottle, he considers drinking but decides not to. He's anxious.*

CRITIC: Fuck you're useless.

DAVE: Yeah, I know, I know.

CRITIC: Do something!

DAVE: Okay. Okay. I'll call my agent … see if I can get an audition for that Shakespeare at the Opera House. No, actually I should check my email first, see if she's got back to me about the ad I auditioned for. No, I'll just find a monologue from *Hamlet* and start learning it, no I need to go to the gym, or should I do a self-tape for that new casting director, maybe I'll write a one-man show … actually fuck it, I'll just do my washing.

CRITIC: Maybe you should start with a shower, you haven't had one for three days.

DAVE: Yeah. Good idea.

ADDICT: Or maybe you should just have a line of coke.

DAVE: It's ten a.m. on a Monday morning.

ADDICT: And?

DAVE: I'm not sure it's the best thing for my anxiety.

ADDICT: What do you mean? Cocaine's great for anxiety.

DAVE: No, I need to get my shit together.

*DAVE starts trying to clean and organise his space.*

ADDICT: Look, Hamlet, I agree, I do, you need to get your shit together—it's just more fun getting your shit together after a line.

DAVE: No, 'cause if I have a line then I'll want a drink and then I'll want to have sex and then I'll want another line and then I'll want another drink and it's just endless … and before I know it it's next Monday already.

ADDICT: Hey, where's that bag from the weekend?

DAVE: I threw it out.

*The ADDICT goes looking for the bag.*

ADDICT: Are you insane, that's the triple-A-grade gear from Bondi—what are you thinking?

*The* ADDICT *finds the bag.*

C'mon, mate, we deserve a few lines, it's the last Monday of the week!

CRITIC: You're not seriously thinking of doing lines of cocaine on a Monday morning?

ADDICT: Oh great, the fun police are here.

DAVE: No, he's right. I can't just sit around drinking and doing lines all day.

ADDICT: Um … you've still got a bag here that's hardly been touched, you can't just throw it away. Who are you? James Packer now? You can just throw away three hundred-dollar bags of coke?

CRITIC: You do realise you'll be doing cocaine by yourself, in your lounge room, staring at the wall, at ten a.m. on a Monday morning?

ADDICT: What else would you be doing on a Monday morning?

CRITIC: You're doing nothing with your life, you do know that. Still renting, you don't own anything, getting bit parts on TV, doing independent theatre. When was the last time you achieved anything? Huh. There's always been something wrong with you. You're always doing the wrong thing. You've always been bad, always in trouble, never had any discipline, never been good enough. That's it, isn't it? You're just not quite good enough, are you, Dave? Stop being so pathetic, you piece of shit. Sort your life out.

DAVE: He's right.

ADDICT: Yeah, of course he's right. It's Monday, you have to sort your life out, you do. But right now we got no get-up and go. We just need a little bit of a pick-me-up, that's all. And then first thing tomorrow, we hit the gym, call the agency, find a monologue and you can be Hamlety fucken Hamlet all fucken day long.

DAVE: Promise?

ADDICT: Mate, would I lie to you? Just a teeny-weeny line and you'll get everything done.

*DAVE takes this in. He weighs his options.*

DAVE: Fuck it, let's rack it up. I'll have a line, get a bit of energy then I'll sort my shit out.

*DAVE does a line of coke.*

ADDICT: Hellooooo, Monday! Hey mate, after this bit of rack I reckon we go to the pub, have a couple of beers, have a punt, come back here with a bottle of wine, tell all the girls on Tinder we got the triple-A-grade coke, have a good old-fashioned root, and finish the bag!

DAVE: I thought we were doing something productive.

ADDICT: Yeah, we are. Tomorrow. Alright. I promise. Finish this bag then that's it. On the straight and narrow from tomorrow on.

*DAVE does a bigger line of coke.*

Hey, you know what I love? That other thing we had on the weekend, you know ... the fried rice, the ice. We could have a pipe later, bit of a smoke, go for a cruise up the Cross.

DAVE: I don't know, mate, that shit's pretty heavy. But maybe.

*DAVE does an even bigger line of coke.*

Maybe.

## 4. HELLO? THE CASTLE PART 1

*The little boy's castle.*

DAVE: Hello?
Hello?
Hello?

*DAVE picks up some foil, a lighter and a bag of meth. He smokes it.*

## 5. HER

*A memory. Darlinghurst Road, Kings Cross, the night after Monday morning, it's two a.m. on a weeknight. Busy but not crazy.*

DAVE: I'm walking past McDonald's on Darlinghurst Road and I see her there. She's writing in a book. Kind of looks Bohemian, pretty face. I'm interested because she's writing, it's what I do sometimes—you know, write in a café, like a cool cunt. But she's writing in McDonald's at two a.m. in the Cross.
Hi.
'Hi,' she says back. It's not a rejection, she's happy to talk.
I noticed you writing. Do you mind if I ask what you were writing about?

HER: A poem. About love.
DAVE: Have you got a broken heart?
HER: Yeah.
DAVE: Do you want to get a drink with me?

She knows what I mean. We go to a bar. It's not often you bring this up in conversation, but I can tell from her eyes, so I ask her … Do you ever smoke ice?

HER: Yeah. Sometimes. I have some. At my place.
DAVE: I pretend to be shocked. But I know. I knew as soon as I spotted her.

We go to her place. It's a small hotel room she's living in. It's a mess, clothes all over the floor, shit everywhere. Not that either of us care, we're both in a hurry to get to it, have a hit. She packs the glass pipe and we smoke.

She asks me straight out …

HER: What's a guy like you doing here, smoking this with me?
DAVE: [*to the audience*] I'm stumped. Lost for words. I don't know the answer.
HER: You're running away from something.
DAVE: I'm not running from anything.
HER: Yeah, you are. I can see it. We're all running from away from something. You're no different to me.
DAVE: [*to the audience*] And I'm thinking … I'm nothing like you. So I put it back on her.

What are you running from?

HER: My family. My kids. I don't know what's worse, the fact I love my kids but I can't be with them because of this, or that I don't want to be with them because I love this.
DAVE: [*to the audience*] She's crying as she starts to re-pack the pipe with more crystal.

I'm an accomplice, a witness. I'm part of the tragedy of these kids' lives right now … and I am sad, I'm sad for those kids. I should throw out the drugs, I should put her in a car, take her to a hospital, to rehab, anywhere. That's what I should do. That's what I would do if I was me. But I'm not. I'm not in control. I want to keep smoking that pipe. I want to fuck, and I want it to never, ever stop.

That's sad, I say, still trying to convince myself I'm nothing like her.
You want to fuck?
Yeah, she says.

## 6. THE TAB

*A TAB within a pub, sounds of racing in the background. People chattering. It should sound and feel busy, sounds of poker machines amongst the other noises. It's a twenty four-hour pub in the middle of the Cross, the night after he leaves her.*

BLOKE: Oh, mate, if that horse hasn't been pulled up I'm not standing here! One dollar eighty favourite in a field of six and it gets beat.

*DAVE pulls a 'Best Bets' booklet from his back pocket. The title should be visible to the audience.*

DAVE: Yeah, tell me about it. I'm down to my last pineapple.

[*To the audience*] It's great when you're on a meth bender and can't sleep, you can throw all your money away punting anywhere around the world twenty-four hours a day.

It's three a.m. at the Vegas Lounge in the Cross and I'm having a flutter on the fillies in France. Hey mate, what do you like in the next in … Paris?

*They both start to look at the form guide.*

BLOKE: Let me have a look mate. What about Actingcareer, the top weight?

DAVE: Yeah, Actingcareer sounds good. Any form?

BLOKE: Na, no form, it's a maiden.

DAVE: Yeah, first start, apprentice jockey … Hundred to one—probably those odds for a reason, hey.

*Beat.*

Fuck it. I'm gonna back it.

BLOKE: Can you have a bit on it for me, mate?

DAVE: I'll have a dollar on it for you, mate.

BLOKE: Tight arse.

DAVE: I'm not Saint Vincent de Paul.

BLOKE: You know how to fill out a ticket?

DAVE: Mate, my old man taught me to how to fill out a ticket before I knew the alphabet. Instead of lullabies he put me to sleep with classic Melbourne Cup race calls.

>DAVE *approaches the betting counter.*

Can I have ten doll ... sorry? Eleven dollars on the nose? Actingcareer. Horse one, next race in ... Paris.

>*He hands the* BLOKE *his ticket.*

Here's your ticket.

>DAVE *turns into a* RACING COMMENTATOR, *finds a pair of binoculars and calls a race.*

RACING COMMENTATOR: Stand by for a start. Green light. And they're away, Icouldbeajournalist jumped okay from the outside and away well was Maybeafootyplayer with Mumwantsmetodolaw over near the rail, coming through behind them was Whatabouthearmy, then Moveoverseas, Theresalwaysbusinessmanagement, and with Commercialrealestateinbrisbane second last but on the improve and at the back of the field was Actingcareer.

They head around the side now and taking up the lead is Icouldbeajournalist by a length Mumwantsmetodolaw, Whatabouttthearmy sits third on the rail and has the box seat and outside it starting to wind up was Maybeafootyplayer by about a length to Theresalwaysbusinessmanagement, Commercialrealestateinbrisbane and Actingcareer which is off the fence and looking for a run wide.

Around the home corner five hundred metres left to go Icouldbeajournalist was headed by Mumwantsmetodolaw, Whatabouttthearmy can't go on with it and here's Maybeafootyplayer making a big run on the outside rail, Actingcareer's four wide starting to make a run for these leaders now ...

>DAVE *is now back in the TAB looking at the screen.*

DAVE: C'mon Actingcareer!

RACING COMMENTATOR: As it's put under the whip and found a good part of the track wide, Maybeafootyplayer's a neck in front of Actingcareer, there's a fight for third spot between Mumwantswantmetodolaw and Whatabouttthearmy, but here's one for the headlines ...

DAVE *is now back in the TAB looking at the screen.*
DAVE: Kick, kick, fucken kick!
RACING COMMENTATOR: The hundred to one starter Actingcareer has kicked away and said ta-ta to a Maybeafootyplayer and it'll get the money, to bowl the punters over. Actingcareer is first past the judge, coming in second was Maybeafootyplayer, Mumwantswantmetodolaw will finish third and Commercialrealestateinbrisbane has finished stone motherless last.

DAVE *is now back in the TAB looking at the screen.*
DAVE: You little beauty!
BLOKE: I told ya, mate! I fucken told ya! Stick with me, son, and you'll be farting through silk.
DAVE: It was always going to win, that horse! I knew it. Hey, mate, where are you going? We're staying here till it's correct weight! It's not paying yet. I want my dollar back!

## 7. YOU ARE NOT YOUR DISEASE

*Rehab.*

DAVE: I've been here a week and I still can't get over how lush this place is. Manicured gardens, beautiful pools, outdoor dining halls—it looks like a resort—the only thing that gives it away is the barbed-wire fence.

You do a lot of learning here, a lot of education, a lot of therapy. Every morning it's process group, then you'll have a mindfulness class like meditation, then a lecture on addiction, then a psych class, then a specialty group based on a cross-addiction like shopping. There are people in rehab with shopping addictions, I shit you not.

I'm waiting for my first one-on-one with my counsellor. He's around the corner having a cigarette, they all smoke, these counsellors, we all smoke too—that's the one thing we're allowed to do. I'm up to a pack a day. I have three cigarettes in the morning before the gym.
COUNSELLOR: David, hi, sorry I'm late. So you're a week sober. Congratulations. How does it feel?
DAVE: I don't know, I just feel angry all the time.

COUNSELLOR: Well, that's pretty normal, just feeling things you haven't felt in a while.

*Beat.*

I see you're not going to meetings in the evenings, what's going on?

DAVE: I don't like them, I don't know why at the start of these meetings we have to introduce ourselves as addicts.

COUNSELLOR: Are you an addict, David?

DAVE: No.

COUNSELLOR: Why are you here then?

DAVE: I don't know. Things just got a bit out of control.

COUNSELLOR: I'm interested—Have you ever tried to stop drinking or using drugs by yourself?

DAVE: Yeah.

COUNSELLOR: How long did you last?

DAVE: Ninety days.

COUNSELLOR: And … what happened?

DAVE: I celebrated.

COUNSELLOR: How?

DAVE: A bottle of vodka and two bags of coke and three hookers.

*Beat.*

COUNSELLOR: David, the first step to getting better is admitting we have a problem. It's completely normal to be in denial. I was in denial for a long time myself.

DAVE: I'm not in denial of anything.

COUNSELLOR: Why can't you say it?

DAVE: It feels like we're all reinforcing this idea of ourselves as addicts. We're just adding to the stigma.

COUNSELLOR: You feel there's a stigma attached to it?

DAVE: Yeah, of course there is, it's not like I could ring any of my friends and say, hey mate, I need to tell you something, I'm really struggling with my mental health and I'm taking drugs and drinking every day and I need a bit of help.

COUNSELLOR: So you felt like you couldn't reach out to your friends or family because of the stigma attached to your addiction. The shame?

DAVE: Yeah.

COUNSELLOR: So you were in active addiction?

DAVE: Yeah.

COUNSELLOR: So you're an addict?

DAVE: No, I wasn't ... I'm not ... I'm not an addict.

*Beat.*

COUNSELLOR: Have you ever considered there is power in owning your story? That there is a power in admitting you're powerless? There is power in owning up to who you are? Can you own up to who you are, David?

*Beat.*

David, addiction is a complicated subject, but all the research is there to support the fact that it's a disease.

DAVE: A disease?

COUNSELLOR: Yeah, it's chronic and progressive. It can't be cured but it can be treated, and it gets worse over time. Or you could just look at it as an unhealthy coping mechanism for dealing with feelings you can't understand or don't want to face ...

DAVE: What are you trying to say?

COUNSELLOR: David, there are many reasons why people fall into addiction. I don't think you even understand why you use.

Let me ask you this. If I said you had to live the rest of your life sober, how would you feel?

DAVE: I don't know ... scared of missing out.

COUNSELLOR: On what?

DAVE: Never being high again. Not enjoying life.

COUNSELLOR: Are you enjoying life at the moment, David? Is a life of using paying off for you?

DAVE *is silent.*

COUNSELLOR: Back home, do you feel connected to anyone? Do you feel connected to the world around you?

DAVE *shakes his head.*

COUNSELLOR: What about your work? Does that give you any sense of connection?

DAVE: Yeah. When I'm onstage in front of an audience, that's ... when I'm connected.

COUNSELLOR: You reckon this acting gig is any good for you? All the rejection actors face?
DAVE: Probably not. I just don't want to do anything else.
COUNSELLOR: Okay, well, if that's your passion, fair enough. But no-one is going to employ you in active addiction, David. They can see it a mile away.
So instead of being on stage, you're here in rehab. Is this who you dreamed of becoming? Is this where you dreamed of being?
DAVE: No.
COUNSELLOR: I didn't think so. How long have you been using for, David?
DAVE: Twenty-six years.
COUNSELLOR: And how long have you been using for every day?
DAVE: I don't know, the last two years.
COUNSELLOR: You've been using every day for the last two years and you won't call yourself an addict?

*Silence.*

Why have you been using every day?
DAVE: I don't know.
COUNSELLOR: Do you want to find out?
Do you believe in yourself, David?
Do you value yourself? Do you value your life?

DAVE *is silent.*

Do you like yourself, David? Even just a little?

DAVE *is silent.*

So you don't believe in yourself, you don't value yourself, you don't like yourself, your inner critic and your addiction run your life. Do you think it's a good way to live?

*Beat.*

Do you even want to get better, David, or am I just wasting my time?

*Beat.*

Do you want my help to get better?
DAVE: Yes.
COUNSELLOR: Well, I can't help you unless you admit you have a problem. Just say it, David.

DAVE *won't budge.*

David, I still go to meetings every day, I'm in my twentieth year of recovery and I say it, every time.

DAVE: You're twenty years sober?

COUNSELLOR: Yes, David, I am and I actually give a shit about what I do here and I can see you're just another relapse waiting to happen, another patient too scared to admit they have a problem and before you know it you're back in Sydney using, wasting your life and I'll still be here working with people who actually want to get better. David, when you're fifty years old, you'll wake up one day and ask yourself what the fuck happened to your life. I can't help you because you won't help yourself. I'll assign you to someone else. You can start your counselling all over again with someone new.

*The* COUNSELLOR *gets up to leave.*

DAVE: Okay, I'm an addict.

*Pause. The* COUNSELLOR *sits back down.*

COUNSELLOR: Good. That's a start. Here's a list of the meetings we have available in the evenings. I want you to tell me which ones you'll be going to.

DAVE: Ummm ... Alcoholics Anonymous on Monday night, Gamblers Anonymous Tuesday night ... Wednesday night Narcotics Anonymous, Crystal Meth Anonymous on Thursday and Sex and Love Addicts Anonymous Friday nights. That should cover me.

COUNSELLOR: You're going to be a very busy boy, David. How's that list coming along, things you like about yourself?

DAVE: It's not.

COUNSELLOR: That's okay. It might take a bit of time. Say it again. Say it properly.

*He signals* DAVID *to get up.*

DAVE: My name is David and I am an addict.

COUNSELLOR: See. Easy. Well, more will be revealed.

DAVE *goes to leave.*

Oh, David, before you go I need you to remember something. You are not your disease ... and don't forget to listen to the sweet song of the birds in the morning and look at the butterflies too, would ya, they're beautiful.

DAVE: I go back to my room, I lie on my bed, I stare at the ceiling and I think.

## 8. NO MARLON BRANDO

*The scene starts in the world of the couch and seamlessly moves into a waiting room at a casting agency, and the final phone conversation is at a train station. The phone rings.*

DAVE: It's my agent! Hi Melanie.

Oh … I didn't get the ad. They wanted someone tall and good-looking. Okay. Hold on, let me check. No, I don't have six-pack yet. No, I haven't lost weight since you last called … Well, looks like I won't be in *Spartacus* then. Is that why you're calling? Oh, they want to see me for another ad? Awesome, what's it for? Mortein! Okay, that's easy, I can spray a can. What? A talking cockroach? As in I'll be in like a cockroach suit? Okay. They're looking for a comic performance. Yep, well that makes sense.

[*To the audience*] I can do comic, I'm fucken funny.

Okay yep, I'll check my email after I get off the phone. Oh, Melanie, before you go there's a Shakespeare I'm really interested in auditioning for—

*We hear a dead phone. She's gone.*

I'd love to be able to say no to this audition, but I'm broke so I can't, even if I am being asked to dress in a cockroach suit and pretend to die from a massive can of Mortein on national TV for fifteen hundred dollars. Before tax.

Those three years studying Shakespeare at drama school are really coming in handy.

I'm sitting in the waiting area at the casting agency. I'm early as always. They're never running on time, but no matter what the audition is for, Cockroach or King Lear, I'm always early and I'm always prepared.

And it's always the same people.

The short, bald bloke, the gym junkie, the drama school graduate and the serious actor reading Chekhov.

Then there's the tall, good-looking guy sitting next to me, he just happened to get out of bed looking beautiful. The casting agent always calls in at least one model just in case everyone else is too regular-looking and the advertising agency decide they just want someone, you know, pretty.

And so I wait. And wait. And wait … And I've been waiting for an hour. Now this is totally unacceptable, totally unacceptable, and unprofessional, but I can't do anything about it, because I need them to like me. They might be casting for a TV show next month.

Finally my name gets called. I anticipate an apology for their tardiness as I enter the room. It doesn't happen. I am now the world's angriest cockroach.

I'm looking at the guy doing the casting. He's maybe nineteen or twenty, probably doing Media Studies at UTS, he thinks he knows everything about film because he just finished the semester on Scorsese. He's giving off a vibe, this … disdain, for anyone who would lower themselves to audition for a cockroach and humiliate themselves on national TV for fifteen hundred dollars before tax and agency fees.

I want to explode; I want to tell this arrogant, little, sour prick that he owes me and everyone else here an apology for making us wait an hour. That it's just good manners—common courtesy. I want to tell him about the work I've done, where I studied, the night I got a 'bravo', how I've performed on stages across the country, the sacrifices I've made just to be in this room auditioning for a Mortein ad … but I can't, because I'm here, auditioning for a part as a fucking cockroach and I need him to like me. So I do the first take.

CASTING AGENT: Yeah, can you just kind of make your eyes wider when you see the Mortein?

DAVE: And that's your direction from Mr Scorsese over here. Make your eyes wider. So, I do.

DAVE *does this.*

CASTING AGENT: Um, yeah that was good but can we just try one where you're more like a scared cockroach than an angry one?

And yeah, your eyes shouldn't be quite so wide, I don't think cockroaches have eyes that wide.

DAVE: [*to the audience*] Well, what do the eyes of a cockroach do when presented with a can of Mortein? And which particular species of cockroach am I playing here? It wasn't in the casting brief. There are 4,600 species of cockroaches and of those only thirty are associated with human habitats. So am I one of the thirty or one of the remaining 4,570? Yeah, that's right—I do my research because I'm a professional.

CASTING AGENT: Okay, can you just stick your tongue out at him—no, other side—and put one leg in the air like you're about to run away, and just put an arm out like you're about to fly, and when I spray the Mortein I need you to die.

*The* CASTING AGENT *pretends to spray a can.*

Now die!

DAVE: [*in character as the cockroach*] 'Oh, mate, the Mortein's got me!'

DAVE *dies as the cockroach.*

[*Back to himself*] I finish the audition. I feel sick. I demeaned myself. It's not the cockroach thing, I signed up for that, it's because I couldn't ask for an apology because I needed him to like me.

*The sound of a phone calling.*

Yeah, Melanie, it's David. Look, I just finished that audition and they made me wait an hour and now I'm late for work, which isn't your problem, but anyway, I was just wondering if you could call them and politely tell them they can't do that and then not even apologise for it. I'm not being difficult … I'm just … I'm happy to audition for a cockroach, Mel, but not be treated like one. Are you serious, maybe this isn't working out? It's unprofessional for you to call them about it anyway? Is this about this, or is this about me refusing your advances when you got me over to your house under false pretences to tell me you were in love with me and putting me in a really awkward situation? Because I would call that pretty fucking unprofessional, Melanie! Okay fine. I don't want to be on your fucking books.

*The sound of a phone calling.*

Hey, Richard, yeah, look, mate, I'm really late for work, I'm sorry—the audition. Yeah, I know it's not the first time … Okay … No, that's fair enough, you need people who can turn up on time, I get it … Hey, look thanks for the work while it was there, mate … It's alright, I understand. Okay. Bye. *Fuck! Fuuuuuck!*

## 9. PRESSURE

*Dave's childhood. He picks up a football. A nineties rock track plays.*

DAVE: Alright, fellas, bring it in, bring it in. Hey, Aaron, I'm the captain, so shut up and listen to me—alright! We're the St Kevin's Under-Thirteen A's. We don't take shit from anyone. Forwards, we need to hit 'em hard, ruck 'em when they're on the ground, we want them scared to touch the footy. Robbo, you're bigger than everyone else out there—I want you to break someone's rib cage. Backs, you were hopeless last week, you kept dropping the ball. It's pretty simple in the back line, okay, pass the ball to Thommo on the wing and he'll out-sprint the other winger and score. Alright. Everyone got it? Let's rip someone's head off!

COACH: [*voiceover*] Gee, you're an aggressive young bloke, I love it! What's your name, son?

DAVE: I'm David Smith, sir!

COACH: [*voiceover*] Are you Tom's little brother? The great Tom Smith, the mercurial, hard-hitting, silky handed, speed machine Tom Smith! Are you his little brother?

DAVE: I'm David Smith, sir!

COACH: [*voiceover*] Tom Smith, who made his mother and father and family proud, who played in stadiums all across the world, representing his country at the most elite level, with the sun shining out of his beautiful arsehole as he passed the ball with elegance to his outside backs? You're his little brother! *No wonder you've got ability!*

DAVE: Yes, sir!

COACH: [*voiceover*] Now go out there and get 'em …

DAVE: … David.

COACH: [*voiceover*] Yeah. David, Go out there and get 'em, Tom's little brother!

*We are now in the little boy's castle.*

I'm here.
    I'm right here. I'm here. I'm here.

*Dave's childhood. Late at night, the old family home. We can hear voices, the whispers of adults. The voices of the* MOTHER *and the* FATHER *are recorded.*

It's dark and it's late. I should be sleeping but I can't. I sneak out to listen, it's me they're talking about again.

MOTHER: [*voiceover*] What are we going to do we do with this child? He's too much, I can't stand it. He's a mistake. I wish we'd never had him. He needs discipline, you don't discipline him enough. He is six years old and he has no discipline.

DAVE: I'm bad. Naughty. A bad child and they don't want me here. I'm a mistake. A bad, naughty mistake who needs discipline.

MOTHER: [*voiceover*] David, you're up? You should be in bed. Why are you up?

DAVE: Why am I bad?

FATHER: [*voiceover*] Have you been listening to us?

MOTHER: [*voiceover*] I told you he needs discipline.

DAVE: What did I do?

FATHER: [*voiceover*] Go to your room.

DAVE: I'm sorry.

FATHER: [*voiceover*] *Now!*

DAVE: I'm scared, I run past my room, up the hall. My elbow hits a vase. It breaks.

MOTHER: [*voiceover*] What have I told you! You're weak. Discipline him.

DAVE: No, please, please! It was an accident! It was an accident!

> DAVE *cowers, protecting himself from what is coming. There is the sound of a leather belt hitting a child that crosses over with the sound of the door opening into ...*
>
> *We are now in a memory. A theatre space. It's just* DAVE *and the* DIRECTOR.

DIRECTOR: David, hi, thanks for coming in.

DAVE: Thank you for seeing me.

DIRECTOR: So, how are you? What have you been up to lately?

DAVE: I want to give her an honest reply. Um, you know, just dealing with being an out-of-work actor, using class-A drugs and alcohol to cope with my depression and my anxiety and my self-worth, because as a human being it's generally kind of tied in to what you are contributing to society and I'm not contributing much, but I got clean for a few days to do this audition, which is amazing in some ways but not amazing in other ways because all I've ever really wanted to do is be on stage.

But I don't give an honest reply because no-one wants to hear that—so instead, I lie:

I'm really well, thanks, I've just finished shooting a few eps for a web series and … I've started a podcast.

DIRECTOR: Amazing!, So, did you read the whole play?
DAVE: Yeah, I did, it's great.
DIRECTOR: And which monologue have you chosen?
DAVE: The first one.
DIRECTOR: Well, should we hop straight into it?
DAVE: Sure.

*DAVE moves to start his monologue.*

I freeze. The words catch in my throat. I'm thinking now, I'm trying to think about what I'm saying. I'm lost in my thoughts. I'm shit. My work is shit. They think I'm shit. I can't do this. Fuck. Fuck. I'm not connected to anything, my words, my body, I'm outside myself.

I speak but it's a lie. Empty, nothing, it's not real. I know they feel it. I'm pushing for the truth. It doesn't come.

I sweat, my palms are clammy.

I've forgotten the next line, it's all out of reach.

I look up … and I've lost her.

'That was great,' she lies.

*Couch world.* DAVE *drinks, and continues drinking throughout the scene.*

*The phone rings. He lets it ring out until we hear the first of a number of voicemails. They can be overlapped or garbled, as long as we know that there are people in his world who care.*

VOICEMAILS: David, hi, it's your sister, just calling to say hi to my little brother.

Dave, just calling to see what you're up to. Chat soon, mate.

Ahh, David, it's your father here. Your mother and I are just wondering when you're coming to visit. We'd love to see you.

Hi, Dave, it's Susie … Um, you didn't call back after the other night, just wondering if we're going to catch up again?

Dave, it's Frank. Mate, I haven't heard from you in ages. Hope all is okay. Michelle and the kids would love to see you. Call me back, mate. Frank speaking.

*He turns the phone off.*

CRITIC: You know none of these people like you. They just feel sorry for you. No wonder. Look at yourself.

I don't know why you bother turning up for auditions. You're wasting their time. You couldn't get a sandwich, let alone a role. Who'd employ you? Fat, ugly, talentless.

DAVE: Yeah, I know.

CRITIC: You're a joke. Everybody knows that. Your family. Your friends. They all hate you. You just live, wallowing in your mediocrity. You're a bad, naughty mistake who needs discipline.

DAVE: Yeah, I know.

CRITIC: No-one believes in you. You've failed. You're a fucking failure. Nobody loves you. Nobody's ever going to love you. You just don't deserve to be loved. You're better off dead.

DAVE: Yeah, I know!

DAVE *drinks and does a large amount of cocaine.*

## 10. CAN'T STOP THE FEELING

*Rehab.* DAVE *approaches the* COUNSELLOR—*he is visibly disturbed.*

DAVE: I want to go. I want to go home and get on with my life. I'm losing my mind here. It's like being in prison. A very luxurious prison, don't get me wrong. I'm going to miss the buffet every day, and people washing my clothes, and the pool, and the coconut smoothies, but I'm good. I've learned heaps, I can see how I've fucked my life with drugs and alcohol … I'm just … I'm going crazy in my room staring at the ceiling all the time thinking, thinking, thinking. I want my phone, I want wi-fi, I want my laptop, and I can't believe I'm saying this but I want to look at Facebook. I actually really, really want to check my Facebook.

COUNSELLOR: Have you noticed how green and alive the plants are around here?

DAVE: Are you serious?
COUNSELLOR: Yeah, I am. It sounds like you just want to distract yourself from what you're—
DAVE: Of course I want to distract myself!
COUNSELLOR: Why? What are you feeling?
DAVE: Everything, all at once. Frustration, anxiety, shame, guilt, fear, sometimes it's this deep, deep sadness and I can't ... I just can't anymore.
COUNSELLOR: So, you've been here a month and you're really starting to feel all the things you weren't feeling while you were using.
DAVE: Yeah, all the fucking time, all day, every day.
COUNSELLOR: And if you were home and these feelings were coming up, what would you do?
DAVE: Use—I know. I'd use, but I'm cool now, I'm good. Thanks, rehab. I'm recovered—time to go.
COUNSELLOR: [*laughing*] You're recovered? You haven't even started your recovery, David.
DAVE: I'm glad you think it's funny. Can you just discharge me please?
COUNSELLOR: I can, I can. But before I do, I'm interested, have you been feeling angry lately?
DAVE: No, the anger's gone, it's just everything else. Can we just ... What do I need to sign?
COUNSELLOR: Just a simple form, I'm getting it for you.
So, the anger has gone? You allowed yourself to feel it, move through it and it's passed.
DAVE: If you want to put it like that. Just book the ticket for me. You've got the credit card details.
COUNSELLOR: If the anger's gone, do you think it's possible that in time these other feelings will go as well?
DAVE: Look, I know you're stalling, can we just do what we need to do?
COUNSELLOR: Just follow me to the office, David. Don't forget thoughts and feelings are like clouds, David, they come—and then they go if you don't hold onto them. How long were you booked to stay for?
DAVE: Eight weeks.
COUNSELLOR: And you're only halfway through. You sure you want to go?

DAVE: Yes.
COUNSELLOR: You need to learn to feel without using, David, I don't think you've developed the ability to do that yet. Don't forget, when you numb negative feelings you also numb the possibility of feeling joy, or happiness. You don't get to choose which feelings you numb.
DAVE: I'm not going to pick up.

   *Beat.*

COUNSELLOR: David, you don't even know why you're feeling what you feel. You don't know where these feelings are coming from. How can you possibly say you won't use?
DAVE: I'm not going to use.
COUNSELLOR: [*filling out a form*] You know, you live in your head. Take notice of the world around you. There is a reason this place is surrounded by trees and gardens. All things are connected.
DAVE: Yeah, well, I'm connected to the ceiling in my room at the moment. It's all I do. Stare at the ceiling thinking about all the fucked-up things I've done, all the people I've let down, and I get it now and I'm ready to go.
COUNSELLOR: If you want to distract yourself from your discomfort, why not look at the butterflies and be in awe of the perfection of the colours and patterns on their wings.

   *He hands* DAVE *the piece of paper.*

DAVE: Can you please stop talking about the fucking butterflies?!

   *Beat.*

COUNSELLOR: Do you have a favourite place David?
DAVE: What?
COUNSELLOR: It's a pretty easy question. A favourite place. Somewhere you go where you feel at peace?

   DAVE *searches.*

DAVE: The ocean I guess. I love swimming in the ocean. Always have, since I was a kid. Catching waves, the sound of the surf crashing, the salt … even just sitting looking at the water disappear into the horizon.

   *Silence.*

COUNSELLOR: How long since you've had a swim in the ocean?

DAVE: I can't remember.

COUNSELLOR: Well let me tell you something. If you keep going the way you are there won't be any more ocean swims. You're here for a reason David. You're here because if you're not here you're either in hospital, jail, or you're dead. And I promise you this, if you can get through this, if you can stay clean, the next time you have that swim it will be the most glorious thing you've ever experienced.

Would you like to swim in the ocean again, David?

*DAVE is taken aback.*

You need to be comfortable with discomfort. All people want to do in this world is distract themselves from their discomfort, and as an addict that's dangerous. You need to do the work David. Do the work.

*He puts down the piece of paper.*

I think we'll just leave this here for now, shall we? In the meantime, your prescription: look at the butterflies, listen to the birds. More will be revealed.

DAVE: I go back to my room, I lie on my bed, I stare at the ceiling and I think.

## 11. PETER PAN

*Dave's childhood. He's on stage as a young boy, it feels warm and colourful.*

DAVE: Ha ha! Peter Pan. You're dead!

The very first play I was in, I was probably about ten. I played Captain Hook in a play about Peter Pan. I remember the sword fight. Three steps forward, three steps back.

*He does the sword fight with sound effects.*

You're no match for me, Peter Pan! I'm Captain Hook!

No! Peter Pan! You've killed me!

And then I got to die on stage. It was awesome.

*He dies.*

I don't have many memories from my childhood but I remember that.

Then the weirdest thing happened at the end of the play—this old man came up to my mother and said your son is going to be an actor. I'll never forget it. I was seen. It was mine, a thing that belonged to me. This was the moment I knew what I wanted to do. I remember that moment vividly because it brought me something I hadn't felt up until that point in my life—joy.

## 12. PARTY FOR ONE

*Couch world. The place is a mess. More bottles and associated junk.* DAVE *does a line of coke.*

ADDICT: Okay, let's get set up here. Windows down, curtains closed, door shut. Kings in our castle. May as well have another one.

*He does a line of coke.*

Ah fuck, that's better. He's always on point, that bloke from Bondi.

*He has another line.*

Should we go down the Cross and get amongst it? Just tell all the girls we've got a heap of gear and have a ménage à trois?

*He has another line.*

Actually, no, fuck that—this is a party for one!

*The* ADDICT *swills from the vodka bottle. He's high. He puts some music on, it's Joy Division—'Love Will Tear Us Apart Again'. He starts to sing and mime and dance—he is having a great time. As he dances he pours a ridiculously large bag of cocaine all over himself.*

Oh no, I had it all. Shit, we got none left. Shit.

*We hear a strong, thumping heartbeat—*DAVE *is high—he's done so much coke he feels like his heart could explode—the* ADDICT *still wants more, he starts looking in pockets in clothes. He finds a bag of meth.*

Have a look what I found. I knew we had some somewhere. Get the pipe. C'mon, let's do it!

DAVE *takes a drink.*

DAVE: No. Fuck off. We've had enough.

ADDICT: You know what, you are really, really selfish, Dave. I just went through all your pockets looking for drugs for you and you won't even let me have a twirl.

DAVE: No—let's just get another bag of coke or some more vodka, or go down the Cross like you said.

ADDICT: No. I think I prefer our little party for one, mate. What you need to understand is that I'm the only person in the world that cares about you. And I'm telling you that I want to smoke some fucken ice!

DAVE: I don't want to get hooked. It's been a bit much lately, you know.

ADDICT: [*laughing*] Hooked? C'mon, mate, you're a bit past that now, you're pretty fucken hooked. You were smoking meth in your parents' bathroom last week.

DAVE: But I mean we can stop, right? Any time?

ADDICT: Oh yeah, yeah we can stop, for sure. Totally. Just one last one. Then that's it. I'm here for you, mate. This is good for us.

DAVE: This is the last time, yeah?

ADDICT: [*laughing*] Yeah, this is the last time.

*The lights slowly focus in on the small bag of meth that* DAVE *is carrying.*

## 13. THE ICE STORM

*The scene takes us from the couch world into the hustle and bustle of the city's busy red light district. There are car horns beeping, shouting, laughter, fighting, all at once. It should feel like a sensory overload, in stark contrast to the psych ward where he eventually ends up later in this scene. In the psych ward we should hear smaller sounds of a lady crying, doctors chatting, someone talking to themselves.*

*He stares at the bag of drugs. He gets his 'kit', a little box where he keeps his ice-using paraphernalia. He goes through the ceremony of preparation: he takes out his lighter and places it next to him, he cleans the pipe using a cut-off straw, he gets the drug out of the bag.*

DAVE: The rock. The crystal. You've got no idea what it's like. You see, you have this little bit of clear substance that weighs nothing. Nothing. Then you put it in this glass pipe, and it makes a sound. The tiniest little sound, you have to listen, and I do, I listen. This clink. Wait for it.

*He puts a rock into the pipe.*

Clink.

There you go, and you see it, you see this little bit of crystal and you know what it's about to do ... you know you're going to see it melt and then you get your lighter and you press the little wheel and it too makes a sound ... a different sound, so then you have two sounds, like clink, ssssh, and you hear the gas and you see the flame and you watch the crystal so now you have the sounds and the visuals and then you get these little butterflies in your stomach because you know what's about to happen. So now you have the sounds, the visuals and the feeling ... this feeling of excitement and relief because you know everything is about to go away.

You want to hold that moment for ages. You just hold that lighter far enough away from the pipe for as long as you can so you can see it and watch it and allow the butterflies to grow and then eventually you can't hold it anymore.

You put it closer and then it starts to happen, it starts, and it's so exciting seeing the crystals melt, especially if it's good gear, the hectic gear they call it—and when it starts to boil it makes another sound and then, just as it starts to smoke you put your mouth to the pipe and you know that now ... now it's coming and soon everything will dissolve, like it's never even been there before, like all the world just slips away. Then you inhale it, and as soon as you feel that smoke in your mouth and you start to twirl that pipe ...

My God. My God, do you feel good ... because your brain, see, your brain releases all this dopamine. The feel-good chemicals you know, but it releases heaps of it, like heaps, like so much and you keep smoking it, you keep twirling the pipe to keep it alive, keep it smoking you know, and you want to save a bit, you know ... for later ... and you mean it, I'll have the rest later you say to yourself, but you can't ... you want it all and you want it all now and then you have more and then you have more and more and more and more and then, *fuuuuuck*, you are high as fuck.

So high, you know, and it feels like heaven. And you just sit with it for a bit, just sit feeling good, letting everything dissolve, and I lose myself ... I forget myself.

But now, now you need to move 'cause you're wired, heaps of

energy and you're feeling good, you feel amazing and it's time to hit the jungle. The bright lights, the cesspit, 'cause you know that's where you shine, in the madness of it all.

*We're in the middle of Kings Cross now, it's ten p.m. on a Friday night. It's chaotic as it is, but it's heightened for* DAVE, *like he's in an electric dream.*

Then you just walk, you're looking for anything, doesn't matter, more madness, more chaos, further into the cesspit, further into the abyss, further into the darkness. And I'm walking, looking around, looking for the eyes, looking for the ones who are high and I see them—the ones who've had the pain, the ones escaping what you're escaping. I see them and they see me and we both know. Then you see one, you know, you know the one, high, maybe homeless, for tonight anyway and you talk to her, you talk to her because you know you've got a place to stay and she might need a place to stay because really who wants to sleep on the street and she says 'Okay', 'cause she knows you got drugs, and then you're home.

*We are back in the flat.*

And I get more, more gear and we're both high but we don't care for each other it's just the drug, only ever about the drug and the escape and then the sex and, the sex high is, fuck I don't want to even tell you because I know you'll never experience it but I want you to experience it—but I don't—because I don't want you to take drugs so just take it from me the sex, the sex, chem sex they call it—it is beyond, beyond what God wanted us to feel when we have sex because if he did we would all be fucking junkies, trust me, and anyway and then, then, it's over.

Nothing. No money. No drugs. And then it begins. Now I'm fucked because I can't get on. She can't get on, she goes back to the street to find another you, and now I'm alone, and I know I'll be awake for the next three days.

*He drinks.*

Fuck. Fuck! Has to be some here.

*He starts to tear his apartment apart looking for drugs. Looking on the ground, tasting things. A desperate animal.*

Wait. What was that noise? Shit.

Hear that? Hear it?

People in the trees whistling, speaking in code. They're waiting to get me.

Those motorbikes, hear 'em? It's the same person just driving around waiting for me to leave the house. He's just waiting. They're everywhere, waiting to get me. They saw me. They're coming for me. I'm gonna die. They're going to kill me. Fuck. Fuck. I knew I shouldn't have brought her here. She's told them all. What was that noise? Shit, someone's coming up the stairs. Shit. Shit. Stand still. Be really still. Really still. Softly, softly, turn all the lights off. Hide now, quick. Hide under the kitchen bench. They're here.

The door. Look at the shadow, someone's there.

I hide. Squatting under the kitchen bench for six hours. No, it can't be real, he can't be there for six hours.

*Beat.*

Nope, it is—I can see him.

*Beat.*

There. The shape. In the door.

*Beat.*

Fuck. Fuck it. Lights on.

DAVE *puts on a tracksuit top.*

Make a dash. Out the back.

VOICEOVER: [*whispered*] David …
David …
David…

DAVE: And then I hear them, the voices.

Run, run to the street.

VOICEOVER: [*whispered*] David …
David …
David…

*We're back to the chaos of inner-city nightlife.*

I'm in the belly of the beast now, walking around the Cross, there's no going home because they're waiting for me there now, for sure.

There's no going anywhere, they're waiting for me everywhere.

The street, the noises, the sounds, the lights—the cars, the people, the animals—everyone and everything is after me and I'm scared. Fucking scared. I mean I am literally scared for my life. I'm not safe. I am not safe. They're going to kill me.

I find a shop, I tell them the people are after me. Call the cops, they say. No, no cops. Actually, yeah, yeah, the cops. They'll drive me home, keep me safe. Police station across the road—I'll go there. Safer.

Hello, officer! Officer! They're chasing me! They're trying to kill me!

COP: Have you been taking drugs?

DAVE: [*to the audience*] Best be honest.

[*To the* COP] Yes, yes, officer, I've been smoking ice.

COP: Do you owe anyone money?

DAVE: No.

COP: Are you involved in any criminal organisations?

DAVE: No.

COP: Have you been threatened?

DAVE: No. I just know they're after me.

COP: Who exactly?

DAVE: I don't know, people … the people in the trees pretending to be birds … they're after me.

COP: Ah! The bird tree people, hey? Well, they are nasty but not much we can do for you. You can wait here if you like.

DAVE: No, no, can't wait here, they'll think I'm snitching.

So I walk. Where's safe? Busy street corner. Safe there. Too many people for them to get me there. So I stand here on the street corner for hours until the undercovers come, they don't know that you know, but you do, they're all friendly, you know, pretending to be a friendly stranger. *Ha!* There are no friendly strangers here.

He must think I'm fucking stupid like I don't know, like I don't know they're undercover, and they offer to, you know, walk you home, to see if you want to buy drugs. They ask to, get this, they ask to borrow my phone to make a call, but really they want to go through it, but they don't know, you know, that I know, so they ask anyway like I'm a stupid cunt and I say I don't have a phone and they know you're lying but you don't care because they're just trying to fuck you. So he says to me, he says, you're a piece of shit, and I say … I know, I know.

Then the sun, the sun, the sun and I'm nearly safe, I'm nearly safe, I start to head home, no, I remember they're waiting for me there too. Where's safe? Nowhere is safe! The hospital—it's safe—they look after druggos like me, they'll look after me, and I walk there and then the people in the waiting room, the doctors and the nurses they all want to kill me, no they do, they want to kill me.

*We are now at the hospital.* DAVE *explodes at the* NURSE *behind reception.*

I fucking told you I can't wait here! These people are after me, see that guy sitting there, pretending he's a patient. He's going to kill me!
DOCTOR: Hey, what's going on?
DAVE: Who are you?
DOCTOR: I'm a doctor.
DAVE: You sure? You sure you're a doctor. You're working for them, aren't you?
DOCTOR: Who?
DAVE: The people, they're after me.
DOCTOR: No, I'm a doctor. I'm going to give you a pill that's going to help you sleep.
DAVE: How do I know you're not going to knock me out then give me over to them, hey?
DOCTOR: I need you to take this pill. How long since you've slept?
DAVE: I don't know … three days.
DOCTOR: I need you to listen to me. You're undergoing a drug-induced psychosis, and the only thing you can do right now is sleep.
    Do you want to sleep? All you need to do is take this pill.
DAVE: And I'm thinking yes, yes, more than anything I've ever wanted in my life I want to sleep. And I realise even if he is trying to kill me who cares because I'm a junkie anyway so dying can't be much worse … because if I die I sleep forever. And if I just sleep I'll wake up and then I can get high again. So I say, yeah … yeah, I'll take the fucken pill.

*Time has passed. A psychiatric ward at the hospital.* DAVE *speaks to a* NURSE.

Where am I?
NURSE: [*voiceover*] You're in the psychiatric ward at St Vincent's Hospital.
DAVE: How long have I been asleep for?
NURSE: [*voiceover*] Over a day.
DAVE: When can I leave?
NURSE: [*voiceover*] When we think it's safe for you to leave. And you've been assessed.
DAVE: Assessed?
NURSE: [*voiceover*] Yes. Once you've undergone your psychiatric assessment. It might be a few days.
DAVE: I stay in the psych ward for days. There's a woman here, in a psychiatric ward just for anxiety, her husband is by her bed. She can't stop crying. There's others, mainly with severe mental health problems. I'm not sure, but maybe I'm the only one in here for drugs. Whatever the reason, no-one in here is coping with life outside. Someone brings me a cup of tea and a biscuit and asks me if I'm okay. And it dawns on me, I actually like being here, it's the first time in a long time that I've felt cared for.

DAVE *sits next to another* PATIENT *from the ward.*

PATIENT: Hey, mate, what you in for?
DAVE: Um, I guess I overdosed on drugs. Ice.
PATIENT: Oh yeah, see plenty of that round here. You're an ice addict, hey?
DAVE: No, no I'm … I just had too much. What about you?
PATIENT: Oh, I come here a lot. On me bad weeks, you know. I'm schizophrenic. I hear voices in me head.
DAVE: How many?
PATIENT: About twenty maybe, maybe more.
DAVE: You reckon they're real.
PATIENT: Yeah, they're real. They're people talking to me … maybe spirits, dead people, I don't know, but they're real. What about you? You hear voices?
DAVE: Yeah, mate. Yeah, I do.

## 14. AM I REAL? THE CASTLE PART 3

*The little boy's castle.*

DAVE: Can anybody hear me? Can anyone see me?

## 15. HIGHER POWER

*Couch world.* DAVE *is frantically pacing across his living room. The meth pipe is in close proximity and should be represented in a way that it holds power, like a religious icon.*

DAVE *stops and stares at the pipe.*

DAVE: God. Lord. Jesus. Are you there? I know it's been a long time since I've prayed but I'm fucked, Lord. I don't want to pick up again but I will, I will, and um … I've run out of options, so … here I am asking for you to save me …

I don't know what I'm going to do. So, if you're there … you know, please help me. Give me a sign.

*Pause.* DAVE *waits. Nothing happens. He goes to pick up the meth pipe. A loud knock on the door.*

No way …

*More knocking.*

God. Is that you?

FRANK: Oi! Open the door or I'm going to kick it in—I know you're there.

DAVE: Frank, that you?

FRANK: Yes. Now open the door.

DAVE: Okay.

FRANK: Mate—what's going on? I've been calling for the last two weeks since I picked you up from the hospital. I've been on the phone to your family, the boys, everyone's been trying to get in contact with you. You've been smoking that shit again, haven't you? Even after the psych ward—don't fucken lie to me.

DAVE: Yeah.

FRANK: You got a passport?

DAVE: Yeah … why? Are there people after me? Do I need to leave the country?
FRANK: Why would anyone be after you? Your life's not that interesting. I'm packing your shit and putting you on a plane to Thailand, you're going to the same rehab I did.
DAVE: Mate, I can't afford that, my family can't afford it, we don't have that kind of money.
FRANK: I know. I'll pay. I can afford it. I know you'll pay me back one day, I believe in you, mate, you've got so much to offer, you just can't see it.
DAVE: I can't take that offer, it's way too much—you told me how much that place cost.
FRANK: I told you the money is nothing.
DAVE: Frank, I'm okay, I just need a break from the gear, that's all.
FRANK: Dave, I'm your best mate and a reformed addict, you can't bullshit me, you've got a problem and you can't fix it yourself.
DAVE: Mate, I—
FRANK: It's not a discussion, Dave. I'm putting you on the plane. Now, do I need to knock you out or you going to help me pack?

## 16. TRAUMA TO HEALING

*Rehab. The scene shifts through to C Group counselling (which should feel different to the process group at the start of the play) into Dave's room, then through a heightened metaphysical space, and finally back to his process group.*

COUNSELLOR: David, good to see you've surfaced from your room, we haven't seen you for a few days. How you feeling?
DAVE: I got through it.
COUNSELLOR: Good. Means you're doing the work. I've been waiting to see what you'd do, see if you were serious or not, and I think you're ready.
DAVE: Ready for what?
COUNSELLOR: C Group.
DAVE: C Group?
  The room is deathly quiet. I see written in large red letters on the whiteboard the word 'trauma'. The C Group counsellor walks to the board and he writes 'David Smith, Trauma Legacy'.

I can't associate with the word—when I hear it I think of soldiers, refugees, survivors of extreme events. I'm not sure what this is ... I don't have trauma.

'Dad, why'd you take so long to pick me up?'

I'm twelve years old, in the car with Dad.

'Your sister is sick. She's been diagnosed with acute Myeloid Leukaemia.'

I don't know what he means but the word leukaemia rings a bell.

'Is that like the little girl in Hiroshima, the one who made the paper cranes, what she had?'

'Yes, like the little girl in Hiroshima.'

In this moment everything changes. Life becomes serious.

My sister Elizabeth is fourteen years older than me, diagnosed with leukaemia when she is twenty-six years old, she is a single mum. Her son, Dominic, who is four, comes to live with us, which I love because I have a little brother now and I don't feel like the baby of the family anymore.

My life as a young teenager revolves around the hospital system. There are lots of new words, words like cancer ward, radiation, chemotherapy, white blood cells and remission.

When Dad says, 'Your sister is in remission', it means she is okay.

'Does this mean she's better?'

'We'll see,' he says.

Over the next few years I slowly watch my sister disappear. I see her lose her hair, become more frail, with bruises appearing all over her body. I watch her become skin and bones.

I'm in the hallway at the family home. Liz has one of those Nike T-shirts on that says: 'Three hundred and sixty-five days a year—just do it'. She says, 'If I'm still alive in three hundred and sixty-five days, we should frame this shirt.'

She's laughing.

I'm at her bedside holding her hand. She can't hear me or see me. But I know she knows I'm there. A nurse is sitting across from me, I'm not sure what she is doing. Probably waiting for me to leave to turn the machine off. I'm holding Liz's hand as tightly as I can trying to squeeze life into her. I'm fourteen years old, watching my sister take her final breaths, I'm the last one in the room, the last one to say goodbye. The nurse, this stranger, is looking at me crying as I talk to my sister. I tell Elizabeth I'm sorry that all her dreams will never come true and I am so fucking devastated and this nurse she can see me and she starts to cry and I know she is crying for me, more than she was crying for my sister, because she sees death every day but she can see me—she can really see me—this complete stranger—and I know I will never forget her face.

I leave the room.

We wait.

Dad's talking to the doctor, he turns and says, 'It's all over, mate'.

The next thing I know we're outside, my dad, he holds my sister's boy in his arms. This little boy, with tears falling down his face as he rests his head on my dad's shoulder, just quietly crying, and all I can think about is that his loss is greater than mine.

We didn't know how to grieve as a family, how to talk, how to cope. I mean there is no manual for grieving, we all just got on with it with barely a mention of her name. I do remember for a while afterward whenever the phone would ring I would pick it up, expecting to hear her on the other end.

Being by my sister's bedside, holding her hand as she was slowly dying in front of me, the nurse staring into my eyes. That was a real human experience.

*It finally dawns upon* DAVE.

Everything since that day has just felt so unreal. I've spent the rest of my life searching for something to make me feel real.

I look around me at the group and everyone is listening. I'm talking about this in a way that I've never been allowed to before. For the first time ever I am feeling heard ... by a group of strangers from around the world in the mountains of Thailand.

'Why do we have to go up the stairs?'

I'm six, maybe seven years old. I'm at a barbeque at my friend's house ... I know it's his uncle because the other boy says we have to do what his uncle says ... there is set of stairs, we have to walk up the stairs ...

[*As the little boy*] Hello? Hello?

I remember a bedroom ... and a veranda.

I don't remember the man's face. At all. Even though it happened over and over, whenever I was at that boy's house.

[*As the little boy*] I'm here. I'm here.

I remember there was confusion, something must have been said, maybe the other boy said something ... there were adults ... parents ... teachers at the school ... I just remember that we got in trouble for it.

[*As the little boy*] Can anybody hear me?

It was our fault. The events are cloudy but I remember the feeling. I was made to feel dirty. I've always felt dirty.

And I cry. I cry and I cry and I cry. I cry for all the things I've done to myself to just try to be in this world.

I'm floating now, lost, spinning in the air ... I've never told that story.

*As* DAVE *slowly heads back to his room in rehab his 'Trauma Legacy' is revealed as if written on a whiteboard on the stage. The board should be messy, like it's been written as* DAVE *has been telling his story and we should see things such as:*

*Abandonment*
*Seek Validation (sex, work)*
*Trauma Repetition (career)*
*Shame*
*Trauma Bonding (relationships)*
*Trauma Blocking (sex, drink, drugs, food, alcohol)*
*DID (Dissociative Identity Disorder)*
*Dissociation Insecurity (depression, isolation)*

*Core Beliefs:*

*I'm bad*
*My fault*
*Not wanted*
*Must be self-sufficient*
*Not good enough*
*Low self-esteem*
*I'm a failure*

*On the board we should also see circled 'Not protected' and 'Not safe'.*

DAVE *looks to the board.*

I've never felt safe in the world.

The C Group counsellor tells me that, clinically speaking, me ending up in a rehab facility was entirely predictable. I can see it now. It all makes so much sense.

*We are in Dave's room.*

My last night at rehab. My last night of mountain healing.

I've been staring at this fucking ceiling for months, staring for hours on end. Thinking, reflecting, feeling everything.

This is where you really do the work, when it's dark and quiet, and you have nowhere to go but in.

I've spent years, decades—escaping myself, escaping my body, not wanting to be here, not wanting to be a part of this world. Alone, dead in the water. Knowing my spirit has left me.

I want my spirit back. I want to feel myself in this world. I have to know who I am.

Who are you?

Who are you really?

DAVE *is outside himself. A metaphysical world.*

I crack. I open up. I expand from the inside out, the universe smashing me open, breaking the castle I've built around myself. I am a part of everyone, a part of everything, a part of the whole, made up of layers, cells, star dust, constellations, of eternity.

I allow my spirit to find its home.

I have willed myself here, a returning to this place. I'm back in this world ... and in this moment, I accept myself.

*We are now in process group.*

COUNSELLOR: David, I think you're forgetting something. And I can't let you leave unless you address it.

DAVE: It's my final process group, I take in all the faces around me. All of the people who were here on my first day have gone, but it's still the same—people from all over the world, all ages, all backgrounds.

COUNSELLOR: You're like the elder statesman of the group now, David. You have anything to say before you go?

DAVE: When I first got here I thought I wanted to die—but looking back,

I think I just wanted the life I was living to end, and I didn't know how to end it. I didn't choose to become an addict, I don't think anyone does and if we're lucky enough to be in a rehab we can all recover, we just need to do the work. What I've learnt is that the things that I felt, the things that I feel, the things that you feel—they're real—and it doesn't matter what other people think or say—those feelings are real for you, and we're not bad people for finding a way to cope, we just never had the tools to get better.

COUNSELLOR: Thank you, David. Now, have you started your list?
DAVE: No. I haven't.
COUNSELLOR: Okay. Just write one thing before you go.
DAVE: I look at the group, I can't not write anything, I have to show them it's possible to find something you like about yourself.

> DAVE *picks up the notepad, he takes a moment, it's extremely difficult for him. He writes ...*

Things I like about myself. Number one. I stayed the course at rehab.

> *Beat.*

COUNSELLOR: Well done, David.
DAVE: Thank you. For everything.
COUNSELLOR: I hope I never see your face again.
DAVE: 'More will be revealed,' he says to the group and I finally know what he means.

Just before the gates open for me to leave the compound, a butterfly lands on my forearm, I shit you not. I look at its wings and with my new eyes I see the beauty in the colours and the patterns, and it stays just long enough for me to appreciate its perfection.

## 17. JOHNNY

*Now we are back to Scene One. Early evening. Kings Cross, Sydney.*

JOHNNY: Dave, you coming or what?
DAVE: Fuck it. One last time. Let's go, Johnny boy.

> Johnny turns to me and he smiles ... and I ... I see him, I look at the scars on his face, how bent his body has become, the red spots on his arms, the scabs on his legs, his broken voice. He's probably lived a life most of us would never wish upon anyone and is coping

the best way he can. He's not just some junkie to use with or score from—he's not just a means to an end. For the first time I see him as a human being, and when I look at him I see myself. I see his pain, his need to escape, his trauma, the tragedy of his life.
Actually, mate. I'm right.
JOHNNY: You sure, bro? It's hectic.
DAVE: Yeah, I'm sure, mate.

*There's a voice from Johnny's girlfriend down the street, telling him to hurry up.*

JOHNNY: I gotta go, Dave—see you round.
DAVE: Hey. Johnny.
JOHNNY: Yeah.

*Beat.*

DAVE: There's a hundred places to score around here. Why the fuck did I come back to the Cross? What was I thinking? I want to get on! Hospital, jail or dead. I hear my counsellor. Before I even know what I've done I've walked away.

I think about Johnny and I think about how lucky I am—that I had someone that cared enough about me to actually see what I was going through and to help me. One person saved my life. No-one's coming to save Johnny, there's no five-star rehab in Thailand for him, or his girlfriend, or anyone else on that street. In fact, there's no real chance of rehab for them at all. They just live in a jungle that eats them alive—while people point their fingers at them, stigmatising them, making them 'the other', wanting to throw them in jail. You don't need to punish addicts, the hell of addiction is a punishment in itself. Trust me. I know.

Thanks to my time in rehab I manage to stay clean. I'm still an addict. I'll always be an addict. I'll always want to use. I'll dream about using for the rest of my life.

But now I feel safe within myself. No matter what my mind and body tell me, my spirit is stronger.

I think of my sister more and more … she never had a chance to live her dreams, but I do.

*DAVE searches through the books, clothes and rubbish on the set. He finds a shoe box. It looks to be the one thing he has taken care of over the years, the one thing that's been protected. He opens it. Inside is a T-shirt that has been neatly folded. He takes out the shirt and unfolds it for the audience to see. It's the shirt his sister was wearing at the dinner table. It says '365 days a year—Just do it—Nike'. He places it on the stage, like the shirt has finally been framed.*

*We are now backstage in the wings of a theatre.*

DAVE: I'm nervous. I'm really fucken nervous … but nerves are good. Nerves mean it's real.

I'm backstage in the theatre, in the belly of the beast. They've called beginners and I'm here waiting for my cue—it's a sound cue—and when I hear it, I'm on. When the music plays I'm on stage and I can't wait.

I love this feeling. I'm focused, I'm pumped, I'm ready. I'm like a physical, emotional, spiritual athlete and I know that at the end of my performance I will be spent, having left my body, heart and soul on the stage—knowing I've touched the hearts of other human beings.

I close my eyes and take a breath. I say thank you for everything I've been through to get me to this point. This point right here in the theatre tonight. This is what gives me meaning. This is what gives me purpose. This is what excites me.

That's my cue—I'm on!

As I step onto the boards I become taller. I transform in almost an instant. The lights, the sound, the rake of the stage, the feel of the set, the props, the sense of my costume on my skin, lead me into another world, the world of the play. I'm immersed now, overtaken, but in control, and I'm joyous.

I feel the heat of the light on my face and I know the audience can see me.

I'm open, I'm alive, I belong. I'm truly in the moment but I'm so in it I don't know and I let go, I open up and I lose myself, I forget myself, no past, no future, only now … and when I speak on this stage, the sounds I create, the words that emanate from my mouth are all of me—they come from all of me, they resonate in every cell of my body, down to the tiniest atom and the sounds float through the space and as they reach you they fill the room with meaning, and now

I'm connected to every heartbeat in this theatre and I feel you listening. Something is said that is real …

I tried dying and it didn't work … I might as well try living …

DAVE *picks up a towel and sits on the shores of the the ocean.*

## THE END

## www.currency.com.au

Visit Currency Press' website now to:

- Buy your books online
- Browse through our full list of titles, from plays to screenplays, books on theatre, film and music, and more
- Choose a play for your school or amateur performance group by cast size and gender
- Obtain information about performance rights
- Find out about theatre productions and other performing arts news across Australia
- For students, read our study guides
- For teachers, access syllabus and other relevant information
- Sign up for our email newsletter

**The performing arts publisher**

www.ingramcontent.com/pod-product-compliance
Lightning Source LLC
Chambersburg PA
CBHW050026090426
42734CB00021B/3436